My First Day as a Junior Park Ranger

ISBN: 978-1-7370010-2-7

Written and edited by J.D. Ho
Illustrated and designed by Lanot Design
Jennifer Benito-Kowalski, Editor-in-Chief

Junior Park Ranger Adventure Books
JrParkRangerBooks.com
Alameda, California

Junior Park Ranger Kyler looked in the mirror fastened to the wall of his small cabin. He clipped his name badge to his shirt, straightened his hat, and took a deep breath before heading outside for his first day of work.

Kyler had never lived away from his home and his family. He was a groundhog, and he was used to having all the other members of his burrow around when he had questions or needed help.

He was so proud to be a ranger—but he was also scared.
He was worried he would forget important things.
What if he told a visitor the wrong trail directions? What if
there was an emergency, and he forgot who to call?

When Kyler hopped down the steps of his cabin, he caught sight of an owl in the early morning light. The owl came down to perch on a tree beside Kyler. "Ah," she said. "The new ranger. My name is Lyla." She looked crossly at him with her yellow eyes.

"What do you do?" asked Kyler. Lyla didn't look very friendly, and Kyler wasn't sure if she wanted to talk to him.

"I'm the Junior Wildlife Biologist. I track the bog turtles and the bears to see whether they're healthy, and if they're starting families in our park."

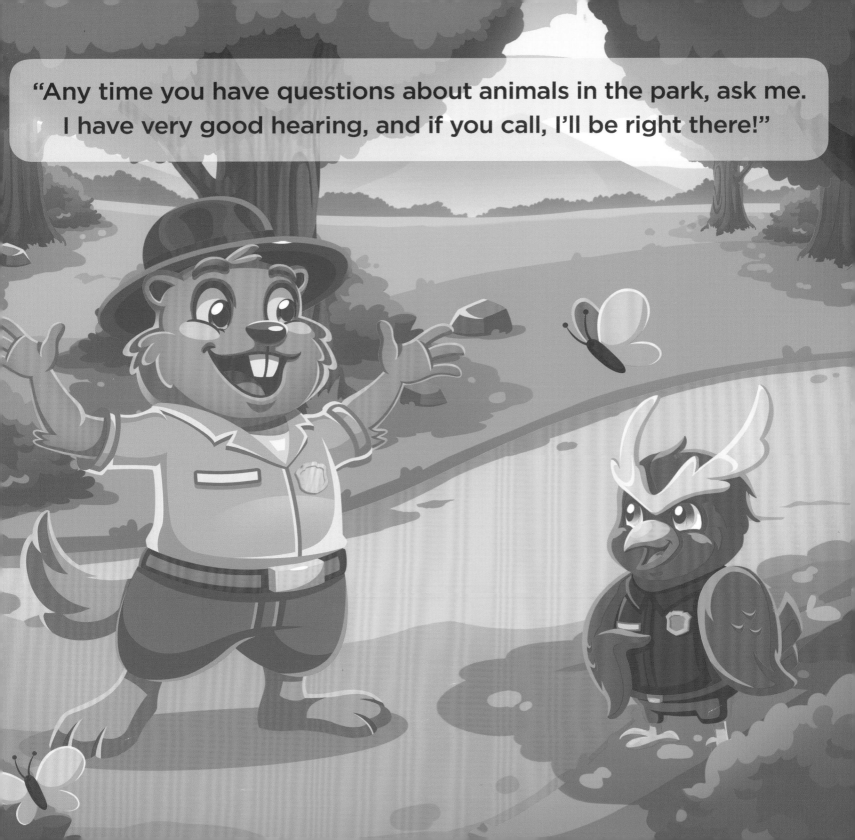

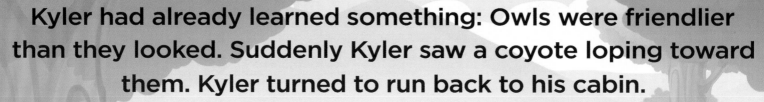

Kyler had already learned something: Owls were friendlier than they looked. Suddenly Kyler saw a coyote loping toward them. Kyler turned to run back to his cabin.

But Lyla wasn't alarmed. "Here's my friend Jaden. He's the Junior Ecologist. He helps me out sometimes, especially during the day. I'm about to go to sleep!"

"One of the things I do is study trees," Jaden said. "We've got a lot of problems with insects, like ash borers." Jaden came up to Kyler and gave him a big sniff. That seemed to be enough for him. He raised a paw in a wave, and then loped off into the trees.

"He had to check you out to make sure you were all right. You got the paws up!" Lyla flew off with a gentle whisper of wings. Kyler smiled. Two new friends! The day was looking up.

Kyler headed down the trail toward the Ranger Station, where he would greet visitors and answer questions. As he walked, he kept a lookout for lost hikers, trash, and injured animals. His job was to keep an eye on things in the park, and it was good to know Lyla and Jaden were looking out, too.

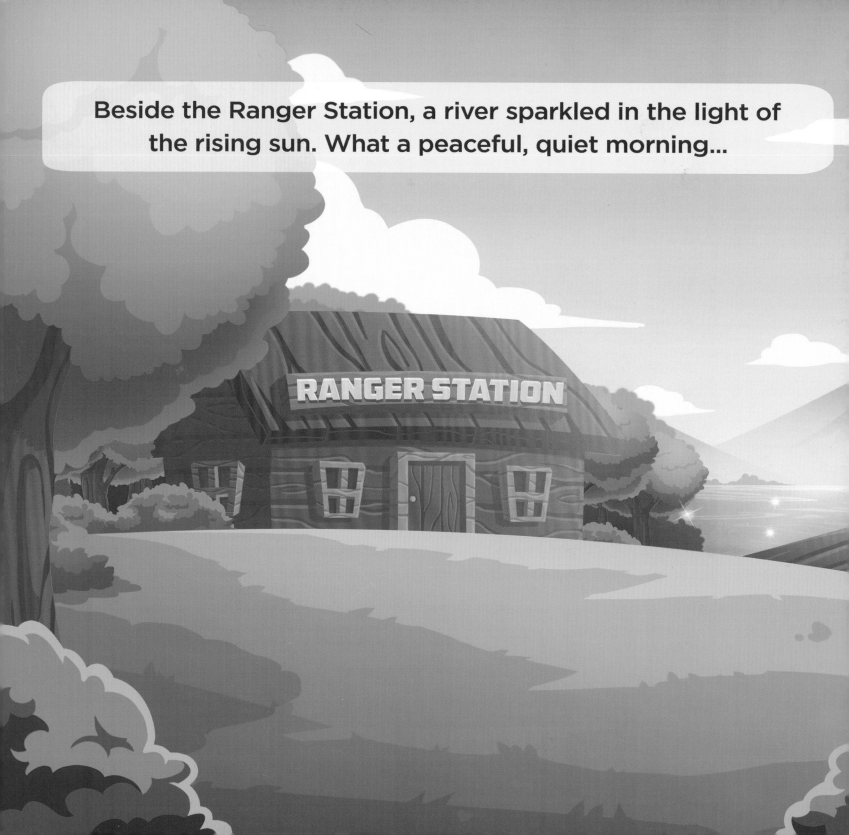

Beside the Ranger Station, a river sparkled in the light of the rising sun. What a peaceful, quiet morning...

SPLASH!!!! Something that looked like a torpedo had crashed into the water. What was THAT? Kyler reached for his walkie-talkie. This was his first emergency, and he didn't know what to do. Where was the lifeguard?

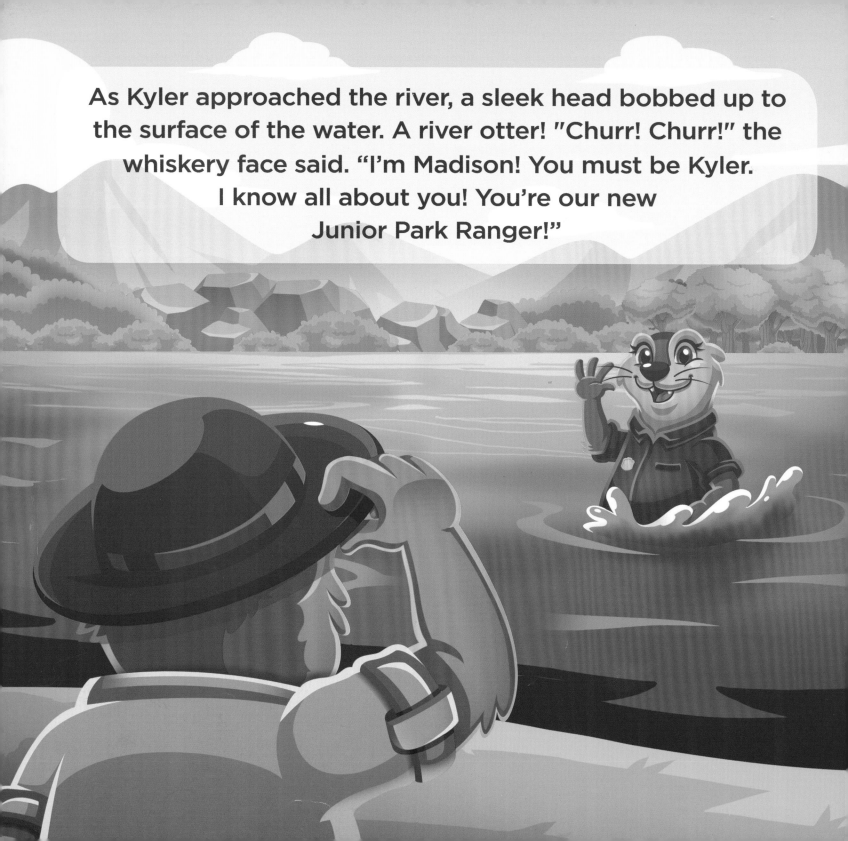

As Kyler approached the river, a sleek head bobbed up to the surface of the water. A river otter! "Churr! Churr!" the whiskery face said. "I'm Madison! You must be Kyler. I know all about you! You're our new Junior Park Ranger!"

"How did you know?" Kyler asked in amazement.
He stopped at the edge of the water.

"It's my job to know things. I'm the park interpreter.
I tell people everything they want to know about the park."
Madison dived back under the water, splashing Kyler.

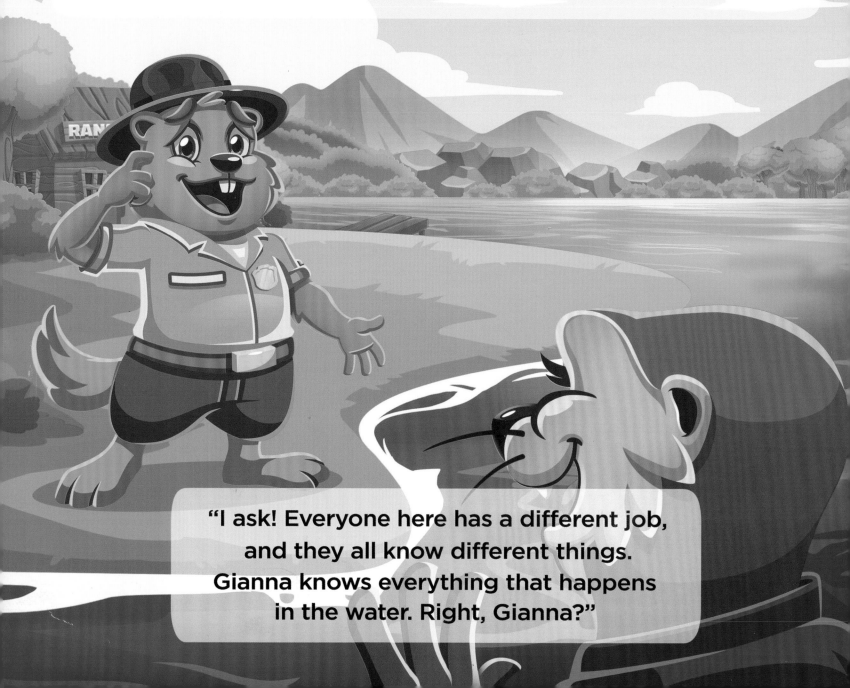

When Madison popped back up, Kyler asked, "But what if you don't know the answer?"

"I ask! Everyone here has a different job, and they all know different things. Gianna knows everything that happens in the water. Right, Gianna?"

Kyler couldn't see anyone. He wondered if Gianna was invisible. But at that moment, a speckled face appeared next to Madison.

"Gianna is our lifeguard. She can see underwater, and if I'm underwater and call for help, she can hear me all the way across the river!" Gianna looked like she was smiling, but it was hard to tell. She disappeared under the water again. "She's a trout," Madison explained. "She's my best friend."

Madison waved a paw. "Have a great first day!"

Kyler thought he might just do that. He spent the morning helping a family from Iowa to figure out which trail they'd like to hike. He handed out maps. He made sure all the dogs were on leashes and that their humans had poop bags.

He checked all the campsites to make sure all the fires had been put out. He collected the trash so bears wouldn't eat it.

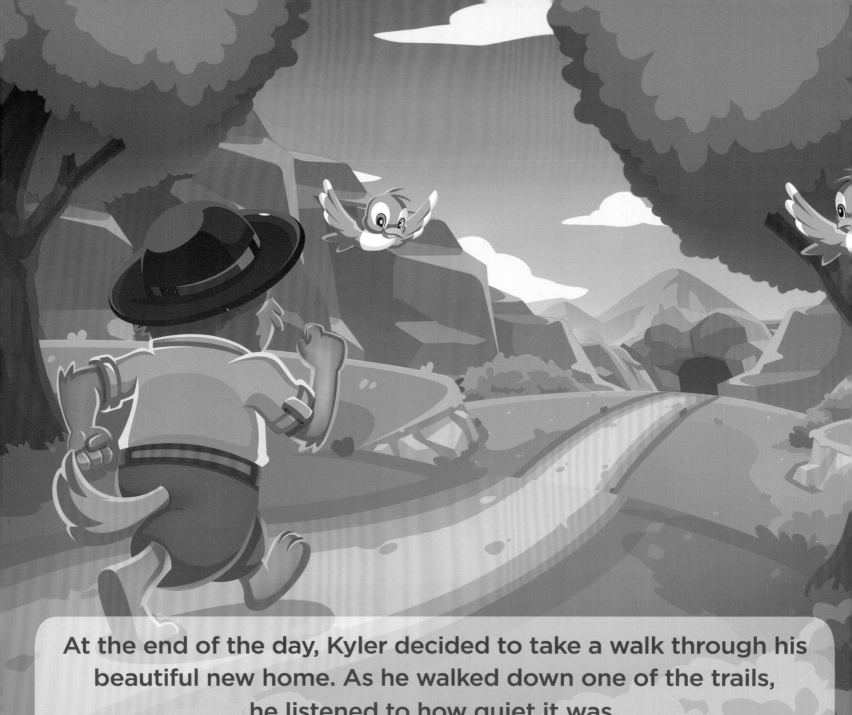

At the end of the day, Kyler decided to take a walk through his beautiful new home. As he walked down one of the trails, he listened to how quiet it was.

There were rustles and chirps, but that was all.

Near the end of the trail, he saw a box turtle lumbering toward him. "Hi," Kyler said. "Do you need some help?" Then he noticed the box turtle's park badge. "Oh, you must be Tanaya, the archaeologist!"

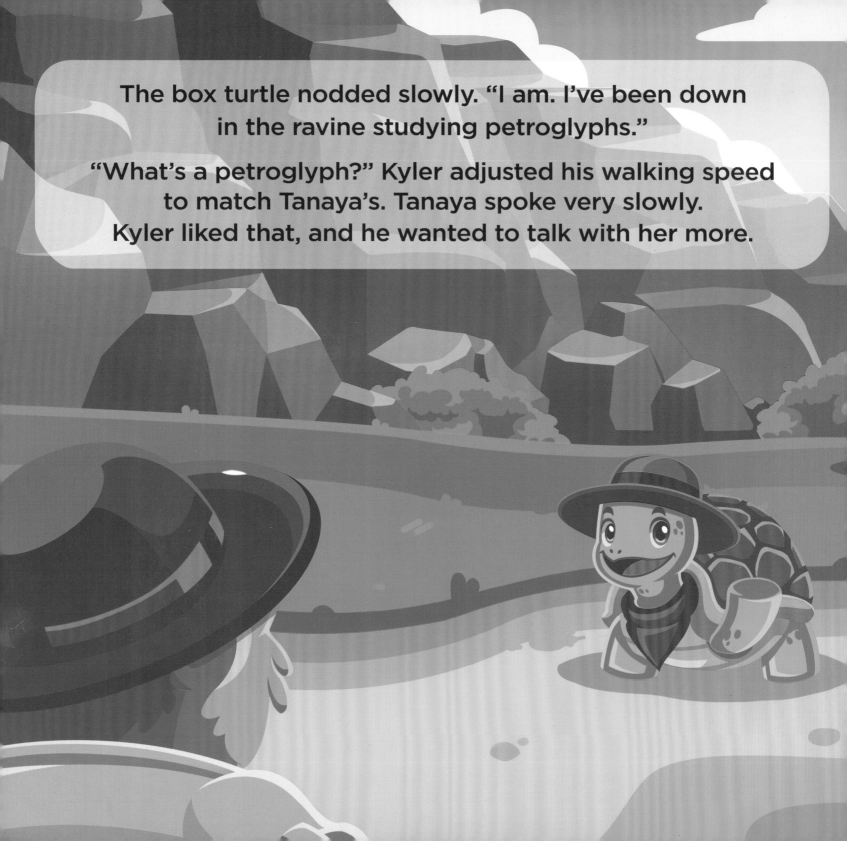

The box turtle nodded slowly. "I am. I've been down in the ravine studying petroglyphs."

"What's a petroglyph?" Kyler adjusted his walking speed to match Tanaya's. Tanaya spoke very slowly. Kyler liked that, and he wanted to talk with her more.

"A petroglyph is a carving in the rock.
This land is old, older than all people, but the people arrived
here long ago. They made mounds out of rocks and soil.
They made these carvings. When I look at them,
I can learn about their lives."

"I've been digging near the petroglyphs to see if I
can find other things those people left behind.
Everyone moves so fast now, but I move slowly.
Like the earth."

The path grew darker while Kyler and Tanaya talked, but there were bright stars above, and Kyler had a flashlight. Maybe part of being a Junior Park Ranger was also walking your new friend back to base camp after a long day at work. Kyler hoped there would be many more days just like this one.

Take the Junior Park Ranger Oath

As a Junior Park Ranger, I promise to be a friend and ambassador to the outdoors and all living things in nature. Making this promise means I will:

- Protect the natural habitats of all living things
- Reduce, reuse, and recycle as much as possible
- Set an example for others so they can enjoy spending time outside, too

As a Junior Park Ranger, I promise to proudly protect the environment in our city, state, and national parks, and in my neighborhood and community. As a Junior Park Ranger, I promise to care for our planet's natural resources, and I will do my best to make a positive and lasting impact wherever I go.

As a Junior Park Ranger, I will always remember that I am a visitor in someone else's (a bear's! a badger's! a bird's!) home. If I don't know something, I will ask, and I will always be kind and gentle because the earth feels my footsteps.

_____

JUNIOR PARK RANGER'S SIGNATURE